SHOPPING CART BOY

Poems of My Life

Joshua Jordan G.H.

Shopping Cart Boy - Poems of My Life
Copyright 2018 by Joshua

ISBN: 978-1-988983-03-5

Published by Siretona Creative
www.siretona.com

Graphic design: Ellen Hooge
Editor: Sheila Webster and Colleen McCubbin
Page 15/16 images courtesy of RT Computer Graphics

Printed in Canada by PageMaster Publication Services
www.pagemasterpublishing.ca

Siretona Creative

Dedicated

To all the kids who have been
taken from their mothers

TABLE OF CONTENTS
DEDICATION

ABOUT THE AUTHOR

SHOPPING CART BOY

The shopping cart wheels
Rattle on broken pavement

I look out of my small metal prison
As my mom searches for a can or two
In the alleys of the hood

By ten we will be at Sarcan on Albert St
Or by eleven on Grant Road
Trading cans for coins
For her cure that never helps

My prison is also freedom
The sun on my young face
No worries of the day yet

Chatting with my sober mom
is much more fun
As the day goes on though
She disappears
Into her bottle - her cure

I am then released to roam until bedtime

As the moon rises
I snuggle close

I love you my son
She murmurs
Between sweet dreams and
Say your prayers

Any day in foster care I would trade
For my shopping cart prison and
Watching the stars and the moon
As my mother snores safely by my side

FOSTER CARE PRAYERS

God of sky and wind
Do you hear my cry
Can you see my hurt
Of being torn from my mother's side?

These people don't love me
Some hurt me so bad
Thank you for the sun and moon
The stars and wind
Who are my friends

But if you love me
Can you tell my mother
How to find me?
Help her to sober up
And find me soon

I don't know how to find her
If this pain doesn't stop
I will find a way to *you* soon

MY REZ PRAYER

God
It's me Josh
I'm hurt again
Can you hear me?
Do you care?

I'm only eight
I hardly remember love
I'm starting to hate

Can you tell
My mom to find me?
Let her know I'm going
To die soon if this doesn't stop

Tell her I love her
I know she loved me

IF YOU SHOULD DIE BEFORE YOU WAKE

I woke up early
Hoping to see you smile
Instead, I couldn't feel you breathing

The joy of having you home
From the hospital
Turned to horror

My own words crying
Help me
Help me
My mom's not breathing!

It was morning but darkness
Came and hid the light
It brought strangers

Police
Ambulance
A social worker

I wanted to run and hide
But I didn't want to leave
Machines couldn't make you breathe
Again

You were gone
For real
Forever

I wanted to die too
I couldn't go back to foster care
Killing myself seemed better

But my brother came
And I shut down as he took me away

8

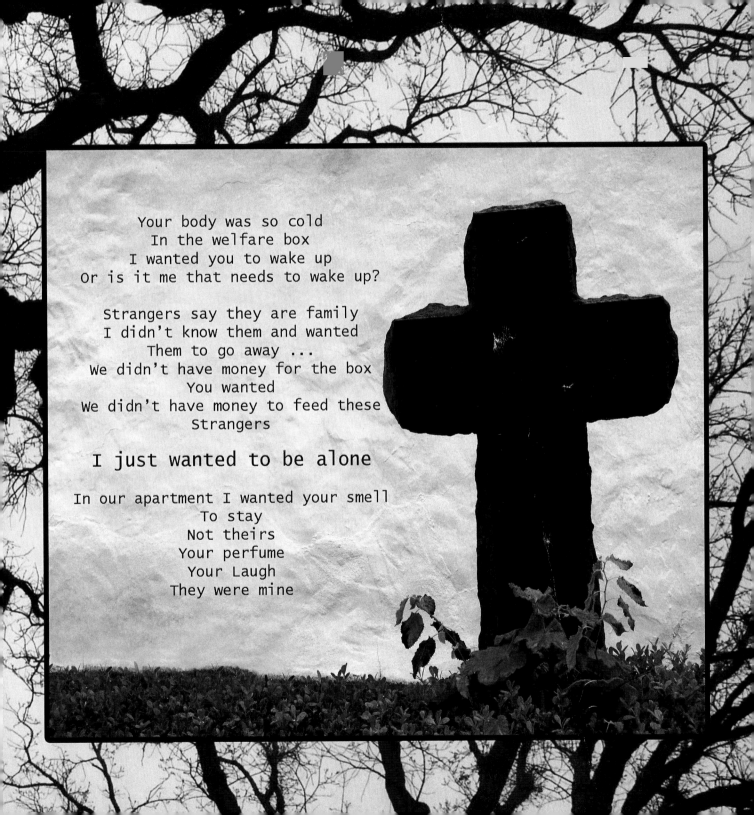

Your body was so cold
In the welfare box
I wanted you to wake up
Or is it me that needs to wake up?

Strangers say they are family
I didn't know them and wanted
Them to go away ...
We didn't have money for the box
You wanted
We didn't have money to feed these
Strangers

I just wanted to be alone

In our apartment I wanted your smell
To stay
Not theirs
Your perfume
Your Laugh
They were mine

The funeral home
Felt like the saddest church day

People wouldn't shut up
They did your makeup wrong
Your casket looked plain
I wanted your star-blanket
On it
To decorate it
You liked blue
And pretty things

***

It was a long journey
To Winnipeg
You went in the back
Of Someone's truck
I kept crying and wouldn't leave the wake
To see you laid in the cold ground
Beside the parents that you loved

There was no one but strangers
To tell me it was OK
Even my brother seemed like a stranger

Having your mom die by your side
Is never OK
When you are twelve

AFTER DARK

The hood is alive
After Dark
People going places
Smoking drinking
Swearing yelling
Trying to feel alive
But only to survive

RUNNING ERRANDS

I'm not smart
But I'm not dumb
I know what an errand means

Delivering to someone
So they don't get caught
Cuz I'm a kid
They say it won't be so bad

I'm scared to say no
What if it means
I'll have no place to go?

If I'm caught
I just pretend not to know
Where I was asked to go

I can say I picked it up
On the ground
I was looking
For the lost and found

Only once the police chased me

My heart was pounding
I was shaking
But tried to act OK

I wished it wasn't my life
But I laughed anyway

BEER STORES

Beer stores make me angry
I feel like they runined our lives
Alive and lying they feel
A white man's lie
It's a party
The ads say
But it's a wake
For my people
Think about it
It's a cure for life
It must be death

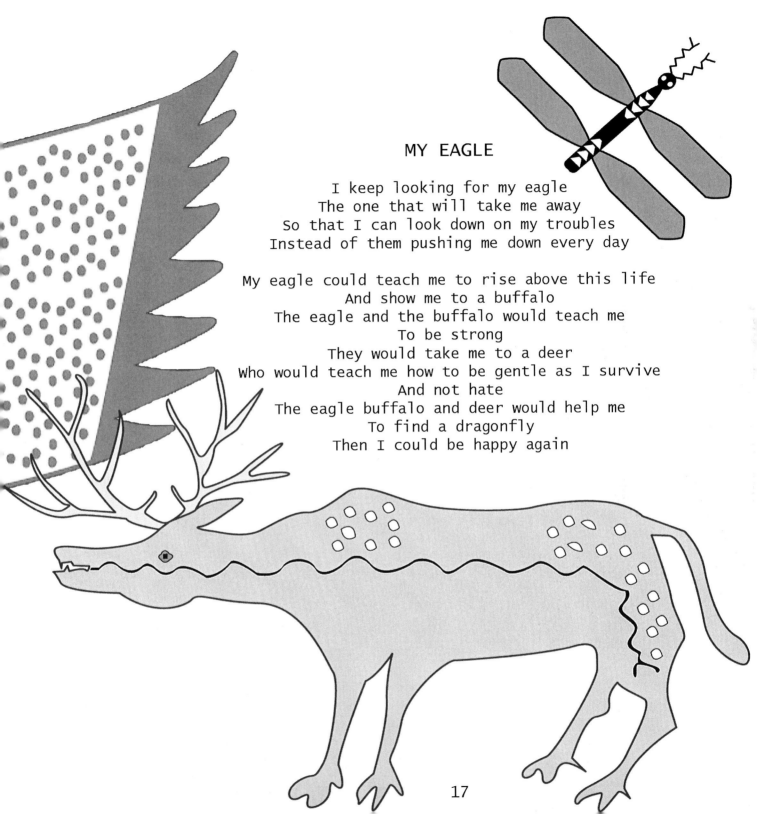

MY EAGLE

I keep looking for my eagle
The one that will take me away
So that I can look down on my troubles
Instead of them pushing me down every day

My eagle could teach me to rise above this life
And show me to a buffalo
The eagle and the buffalo would teach me
To be strong
They would take me to a deer
Who would teach me how to be gentle as I survive
And not hate
The eagle buffalo and deer would help me
To find a dragonfly
Then I could be happy again

A COUPLE GOOD ONES

A couple good memories
That gave me some faith
And the words that said
Don't give up on grace
I'll keep those memories
Inside a good place

Don't throw your life away
Keep it together
Because who knows
What will come your way

Think of freedom
Try to remember
The happiness that
These memories show you
And stay with you forever

EDUCATION

You tell me things I don't understand
You look like you want to show me
That back of your hand
Your words confuse me
I want to learn
But learning isn't easy
When you are trying to survive

You yell at me because I'm crying
My mom died two weeks ago
You say I'm not trying
If your mom died
I would care
But I'm just a kid
From nowhere

I want to learn but this is how ...
Use small words
And be patient with me
Tell me of things I can see
And treat me like I treat you
As a human of worth

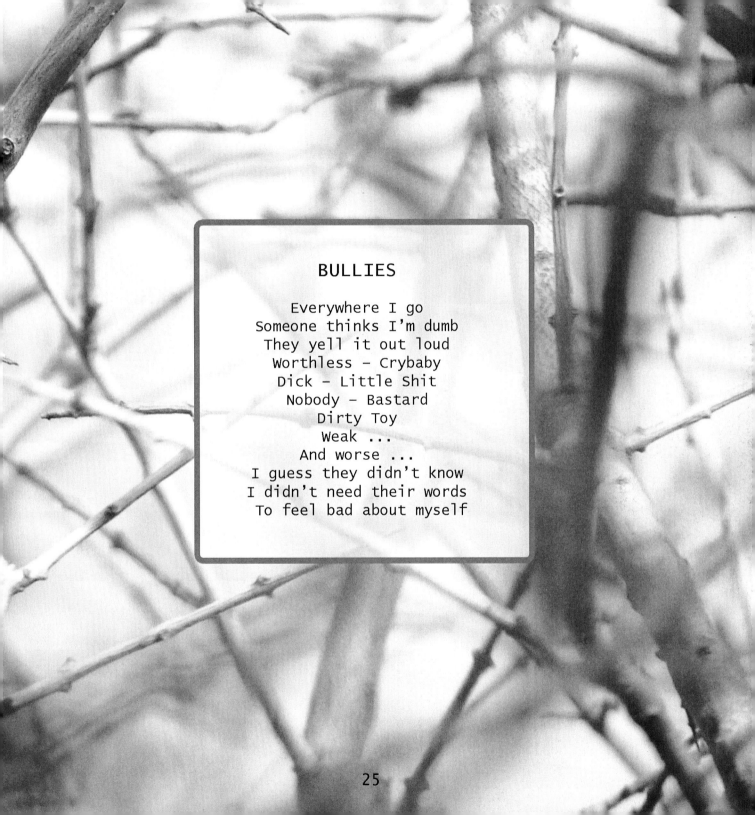

BULLIES

Everywhere I go
Someone thinks I'm dumb
They yell it out loud
Worthless – Crybaby
Dick – Little Shit
Nobody – Bastard
Dirty Toy
Weak ...
And worse ...
I guess they didn't know
I didn't need their words
To feel bad about myself

STREET ROPES

I'm on the streets
Being shown the ropes
Of break and enter
Theft
And running errands
Having a smoke
Sometimes a toke

It's cold out at night
And scary
We are only twelve and ten but
He knows more crime than me

There is always someone
Or something
To be scared of

It feels fun
For some
But deep down
I'm hungry, cold and tired

I wonder if my mom is colder
In her grave

But it's those thoughts that
Keep me running

MY BROTHER

We didn't used to like each other
Then our mom died
I wished we knew each other better
So we could give comfort
And share memories

He would comfort me because
I was her pet and the youngest
I would comfort him because he
Was her pride and Joy
But she
Was never there for him
As she tried to be for me

MY DAD

I didn't know 'till my mom died
Who he was
But I still never knew him
He died when i was three
My mom didn't tell me
I was afraid to ask
I have no picture of him

What did he look like?
Was he tall?
Does my nose really look like his?
What about his other kids?
Did he see me when I was small?
Did he care at all?

When I become a father
I want to be a man
My children will know me
They will hold my hand

I will make them known
Before they are born
I will hear their first cry
And wipe away their tears

I wish I had a father
To keep me from foster care
A father to help my mother
And keep our family together
Because I am here
I know I had a father
And because he gave me life
I will give him honour

I really don't know his name
Or what he was even like
But I will make my life count
So that when we meet
He can be proud

THE CUZINS

Junior and his wife
Are my brother's cuzins
But I don't know if they are mine

When we were lonely
We walked through the hood
And crashed at their house
It was kinda good
But there were errands
I didn't want to run
I liked his wife
I wish I had one

My brother and cuzin
Trouble always found them
It was funny at times
But mostly scary

I wanted to look up to them
But usually turned away
I didn't want to be them
But I had no idea who to be

MY DOG

I needed a friend
To help in my grief
Your fur so soft
Your eyes so brown
A puddle of puppy
Just a few pounds
I loved you a lot
But I had no one
To show me how
To be good to you
When you needed someone
I needed you but
Your needs made me mad
When you whined
Cuz you were hungry
That made me feel bad
I yelled at you
Because I was angry at life
The policeman heard me
And took us both home
But it was never the same
... Again ...

WHY WE DIDN'T HAVE SEX

It's not that you weren't pretty
Or that your skin wasn't soft
It wasn't that I didn't want to
Or that there was something wrong

I just think you only offered
Because
You were hurt by someone
You were looking for love and
You deserved love
But I wasn't the one

When I have sex
It will be with my one
It will be my decision
And not just for fun
It won't be in Dewdney Park
And we won't be just kids
Afraid not to be loved
Or alone for another night

I wish you could see how
I remember you
Your perfume
Your face
Your skin so warm
Your innocence long gone
Undressing in the moonlight

To me you were worth more
Than just one moment
You were perfect
But didn't even know it

My innocence was taken
By a cruel twist of fate
Tortured over and over
More out of hate

I didn't want to add
To your pain or mine
By fusing our bodies
Just that one time

ANOTHER MOTHER

No one knows
The relief
To have another mother
A real one who loves me
And lets me cry
And cry and cry
'Til my tears stop on their own

She teaches me things
And loves me

She listens to the bad stuff
That happened to me
And that I have done
Even when people say
Mean things
About me being her son
She stays she smiles she is my mom

I turn white when I am sick
She turns brown in the summer
People don't talk to her anymore
Because I am her son
But she says she prefers reality
To make belief

My favorite times
Are when we drive
Alone for miles
We look at the prairie sky
And watch the wind
On the trees and water
We point out the deer
And eagles and moose
Coyotes or foxes
We say nothing
For hours
And get home
Late at night
We smile we sigh and say
That was a good drive

She doesn't have any money
For things that she would
Like sometimes for me to do

But we share tea or coffee
In pottery mugs or paper cups
And don't mind sharing
Because it makes us
Strong family
We may not be blood
But we are hearts together
And minds made up to be
A different kind of family

ABOUT THE AUTHOR

Joshua is a sixteen year old Cree boy whose biological mother was a member of the Lake St. Martin First Nation in Manitoba.

When his mother died by his side at age twelve, he asked, after a while, to go and live with someone he knew from years before. Even though this person had been treated badly by his family and their friends, he chose her as his mother. It was because he saw that she had always treated everyone with kindness - no matter how *she* had been treated.

Joshua and his new mother do many things together to help others. They worked on this book together. His oral storytelling of his life begged for a form that wasn't as rigid as some of the other stories he wrote about his life. Joshua has grown to love the cadence of poetry as it more aptly depicts the rhythm in his head as he talks about his experiences both on and off the reserve, in and out of the hood, and in and out of foster care.

Born to thrive not just survive, Joshua shows this through his smile, his care for others and his desire to use all forms of storytelling to help other people overcome.